big NATE

FROM THE TOP

More

adventures from

LINCOLN PEIRCE

Big Nate Out Loud

Big Nate and Friends

Big Nate Makes the Grade

Big Nate All Work and No Play

Big Nate: Game On!

Big Nate: I Can't Take It!

Big Nate: Great Minds Think Alike

Big Nate: The Crowd Goes Wild!

Big Nate's Greatest Hits

Big Nate: Say Good-bye to Dork City

Big Nate: Welcome to My World

Big Nate: Thunka, Thunka, Thunka

Big Nate: Revenge of the Cream Puffs

Epic Big Nate

Big Nate: What's a Little Noogie Between Friends?

big NATE
FROM THE TOP

by LINCOLN PEIRCE

Andrews McMeel
PUBLISHING®

Big Nate is distributed internationally by Andrews McMeel Syndication.

Big Nate copyright © 2010 by United Feature Syndicate, Inc. All rights reserved. Printed in China. No part of this book may be used or reproduced in any manner whatsoever without written permission except in the case of reprints in the context of reviews.

Andrews McMeel Publishing
a division of Andrews McMeel Universal
1130 Walnut Street, Kansas City, Missouri 64106

www.andrewsmcmeel.com

17 18 19 20 SDB 20 19 18 17

ISBN: 978-1-4494-0232-7

Library of Congress Control Number: 2010930552

These strips appeared in newspapers from
August 28, 2006, through April 1, 2007.

Made by:
Shenzhen Donnelley Printing Company Ltd.
Address and place of production:
No. 47, Wuhe Nan Road, Bantian Ind. Zone,
Shenzhen China, 518129
17th Printing—6/5/17

Big Nate can be viewed on the Internet at
www.gocomics.com/big_nate

ATTENTION: SCHOOLS AND BUSINESSES
Andrews McMeel books are available at quantity discounts with bulk purchase for educational, business, or sales promotional use. For information, please e-mail the Andrews McMeel Publishing Special Sales Department:
specialsales@amuniversal.com

**To JDP,
the original Big Nate**

AHHH! THE ANNUAL RITUAL! BUYING A NEW SCHOOL BINDER!

..BUT IT CAN'T BE JUST **ANY** BINDER! IT'S GOT TO HAVE ALL THE LATEST FEATURES!

A REINFORCED SPINE WITH QUICK-LOCK RINGS!

EXPANDABLE POCKETS WITH VELCRO FASTENERS!

YAWN

A REMOVABLE MESH PENCIL CASE WITH A BONUS CELL PHONE COMPARTMENT!

WHAT ABOUT **YOU**, NATE? DON'T **YOU** NEED A NEW BINDER?

YEAH, I GUESS I DO.

WHAK!

I'LL TAKE IT.

Do you recall that night in June
You watched the comet fly?

And can you picture,
In your mind,
That ballgame in July?

Do you remember mini-golf,
And all those putts you missed?

Then how could you forget about
Your summer reading list?

MRS. GODFREY

Peirce

WHAT'S THE PROBLEM, NATE? WHY WON'T YOU SIT STILL?

I CAN'T HELP IT! I'M **HOT**!

FIDGET FIDGET FIDGET

I'VE BEEN WEARING **SHORTS** ALL SUMMER, AND NOW I'VE GOT TO WEAR **LONG PANTS**! I FEEL LIKE I'M IN A **SAUNA**!

I'VE GOT THE WORST CASE OF "ITCHY THIGHS" I'VE EVER HAD!

TOO MUCH INFORMATION, SON.

I MEAN, DOES **ANYTHING** CHAFE LIKE MOIST DENIM?

Peirce

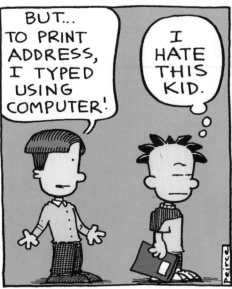

I DON'T GET IT. WHY IS ARTUR ALWAYS SO **NICE** TO ME?

BECAUSE HE'S A NICE KID, THAT'S WHY!

BUT WHY WASTE YOUR TIME BEING NICE TO SOMEONE WHO CAN'T **STAND** YOU? WHAT'S UP WITH **THAT**?

WELL, SOME PEOPLE...

OOP! HOLD ON!

JENNY, M'LADY!

SOME PEOPLE ARE JUST KIND OF CLUELESS.

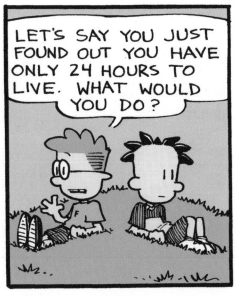

WHY WAS ABRAHAM LINCOLN KNOWN AS "HONEST ABE"? NATE?

HM?

UHHH...

IT WAS PART OF YOUR ASSIGNED READING.

RIGHT, RIGHT...

DID YOU EVEN **DO** THE READING?

YES, I DID THE READING!

WELL, THEN YOU SHOULD KNOW THE ANSWER.

BUT YOU DIDN'T TELL US YOU WERE GOING TO **ASK** US ABOUT IT!

SO YOU ONLY PAY ATTENTION TO THE READING IF YOU KNOW I'M GOING TO **ASK** YOU ABOUT IT?

OF **COURSE**!

UH.. ☆KOFF!☆ ...**NOT**!! OF COURSE **NOT** IS WHAT I... UH... MEANT TO... SAY...

YOU KNOW, THERE'S SUCH A THING AS BEING **TOO** HONEST.

PRINCIPA

Peirce

A goalie, or a "keeper",
(As we keepers like to say),
Is the most important person
On the soccer field of play.

He must make acrobatic saves,
The most athletic kind!

He must be fearless,
Quick, alert, and . . .

Okay, never mind.

34

HI, SCHOOL PICTURE GUY.

AH! WHAT'S UP, KID? WHAT'S THE GOOD WORD?

NOBODY LIKES MY "LOOK."

HMM... I SEE, I SEE.

WELL, THEY MAY HAVE A POINT, AMIGO. THE HAIR-STYLE IS A BIT EXTREME.

I HAVEN'T EVEN SHOWN YOU THE "LOOK" YET!!

OOP. MY BAD, KID. CARRY ON.

OKAY, KID, SHOW ME THIS "LOOK" YOU'RE ALL FIRED UP ABOUT.

OKAY. I THINK IT'S PRETTY GOOD.

I JUST TRY TO... YOU KNOW... ACT CASUAL.

KID, I HAVEN'T SEEN SUCH ACTING SINCE THE HEYDAY OF MR. KEVIN COSTNER.

WHO?

"WATERWORLD." **GAD**, WHAT A WASTE OF TWO HOURS OF MY LIFE!

Peirce

KID, YOU WANT A PICTURE THAT LOOKS GOOD IN THE YEARBOOK? LOSE THAT CHEESEBALL **EXPRESSION** ON YOUR MUG!

BUT... JUST BE YOUR-**SELF**, CHUM! DON'T CHASE AFTER SOME BOGUS **STANDARDS** IMPOSED BY **SOCIETY**!

SOCIETY? PERHAPS A TALE FROM MY **OWN** PAST WILL HELP ILLUMINATE MY POINT!

WHATEVER HAPPENED TO "SAY CHEESE"?

IT WAS RAINING THE NIGHT OF THE "STAR TREK" CONVENTION...

HERE'S AN EXPRESSION THAT **PROVES** DOGS ARE BETTER THAN CATS!

"WORKING LIKE A DOG"!

WORKING LIKE A DOG.

IT MEANS DOGS ARE HARD-WORKING! UNLIKE **CATS**!

CATS JUST SIT AROUND **LICKING** THEMSELVES! BUT **DOGS** ARE OUT THERE **DOING** STUFF!

THEY'RE RUNNING AROUND! FETCHING STICKS! DIGGING HOLES! CATS JUST **SLEEP** ALL DAY!

YOU'LL NEVER HEAR ANYONE USE THE EXPRESSION "WORKING LIKE A **CAT**"!

TRIP!

THERE'S A**NOTHER** EXPRESSION: "DOGGING IT"!

Z

GET UP, SPITSY.

41

I DON'T WANT TO RUN FOR PRESIDENT, BECAUSE **GINA**'S GOING TO BE PRESIDENT.

...AND BEING **VICE** PRESIDENT WOULD MEAN GETTING BOSSED AROUND BY GINA... SO **THAT'S** OUT. ...AND RUNNING FOR SECRETARY SOUNDS TOO GIRLISH...

I GUESS I'LL JUST HAVE TO SETTLE FOR TREASURER.

"I'LL JUST HAVE TO SETTLE FOR TREASURER." **THERE'S** AN INSPIRING CAMPAIGN SLOGAN!

EXCUSE ME WHILE I RUSH TO THE POLLS!

FASTEN YOUR SEAT BELT, SHEILA! I'M RUNNING AGAINST YOU FOR TREASURER!

YOU? REALLY?

YUP, AND I CAN'T WAIT TO GET ELECTED! MY ALLOWANCE JUST DOESN'T GO AS FAR AS IT USED TO!

WHAT? WHOA, **WHOA!**

NATE! YOU CAN'T RAID THE SIXTH GRADE TREASURY FOR YOUR **PERSONAL USE!!**

WELL, **DUH!** I **REALIZE** THAT, SHEILA!

ALL I'M SAYING IS, THE SALARY WILL COME IN HANDY!

UH... MORE BAD NEWS, CHAMP...

HELLO, BOYS!

HI, MR. ROSA.

NATE, I UNDERSTAND YOU'RE RUNNING FOR STUDENT GOVERNMENT!

NO, I CHANGED MY MIND.

OH? WHY?

I JUST DECIDED NOT TO RUN, THAT'S ALL.

HE FOUND OUT MIDDLE SCHOOL TREASURERS CAN'T PRINT THEIR OWN MONEY.

NOT A **LOT** OF MONEY! JUST ENOUGH SO I WOULDN'T HAVE TO HOLD A **BAKE SALE!**

Peirce

MRS. GODFREY, I'M LODGING A PROTEST!

ABOUT WHAT?

THIS "CURRENT EVENTS" TEST! THE WAY YOU GRADED IT IS TOTALLY UNFAIR!

I MEAN, I KNOW I DIDN'T ACE EVERY QUESTION, BUT DID I REALLY DESERVE A C?

LET ME SEE.

HMMM...

MM HMM...

HMM...

YOU'RE RIGHT, NATE. YOU DON'T DESERVE A C.

THIS IS A D-MINUS IF I'VE EVER SEEN ONE.

OH, HOW I HATE HER.

JUST AN F.Y.I: PRESIDENT BUSH'S BROTHER IS NAMED "JEB", NOT "REGGIE."

MRS. CZERWICKI, WHY DOESN'T THE SCHOOL JAZZ UP THIS ROOM A LITTLE?

IT'S SO **DRAB** IN HERE, YOU KNOW? I MEAN, IT'S LIKE A **DEAD ZONE!**

PAINT THE WALLS! PUT UP SOME POSTERS! MAKE PEOPLE **WANT** TO BE HERE!

NATE, MAKING PEOPLE WANT TO BE IN THE DETENTION ROOM ISN'T REALLY THE POINT.

WELL, PERSONALLY, I LIKE A PLACE TO FEEL HOMEY.

HOW COME THEY KEEP GIVING ME DETENTION?

I'LL TELL YOU WHY, CHESTER!

IT'S BECAUSE YOU KEEP REPEATING THE SAME BEHAVIOR! OF **COURSE** THEY'RE GOING TO KEEP GIVING YOU DETENTION!

DOING THE SAME THINGS OVER AND OVER AGAIN AND EXPECTING DIFFERENT RESULTS IS THE DEFINITION OF...

OF WHAT?

...OF SOMEONE WHO IS COMPLETELY, TRAGICALLY MISUNDERSTOOD.

MRS. CZERWICKI, I'D LIKE TO SPEAK UP ON BEHALF OF CHESTER OVER THERE.

HE SAYS HE'S BEEN GIVEN DETENTION FOR NO GOOD REASON, AND I BELIEVE HIM! HE'S DONE NOTHING WRONG!

NOTHING WRONG?

THIS IS HIS DETENTION REPORT.

YOUR REPORT CONSISTS OF THREE X-RAYS AND A RESTRAINING ORDER, SO I'M GUESSING YOU'LL BE HERE AWHILE.

HEY. GO ASK MRS. CZERWICKI TO LET ME OUT OF HERE.

CHESTER, I ALREADY TRIED ONCE! IT WON'T DO ANY GOOD!

YOU SENT SOME KID TO THE **EMERGENCY ROOM**!

HE STARTED IT.

WHATEVER! BOTTOM LINE, YOU PUT A BEAT-DOWN ON HIM! YOU DON'T HAVE A LEG TO STAND ON!

NEITHER DOES THE OTHER KID. HA HA.

YOU'RE A RIOT, CHESTER.

Peirce

WHO'S THIS IN THE PHOTO, MRS. CZERWICKI?

THAT'S MY DAUGHTER.

AND THAT GUY NEXT TO HER IS HER HUS-BAND, I GUESS?

HUSBAND? OH, NO NO! WHY HAVE A **HUSBAND** WHEN YOU CAN JUST **SHACK UP** WITH SOMEONE?

SHE **COULD** HAVE MARRIED **KEVIN**! BUT **NO!** KEVIN WASN'T **EXCITING** ENOUGH FOR HER!

INSTEAD IT WAS: "HELLO, MA? I MET THIS NEAT GUY ON THE **INTERNET!**"

TIME FOR ME TO SIT BACK DOWN.

Peirce

MR. GALVIN? CAN I INTERVIEW YOU FOR THE SCHOOL NEWSPAPER?

I SUPPOSE SO.

OKAY, FIRST QUESTION: WHAT DO YOU THINK OF MS. LA CHANCE?

MS. LA CHANCE? SHE'S AN EXCELLENT TEACHER.

SO YOU LIKE HER!

YES, SHE'S A VERY NICE PERSON.

GOOD HEADLINE! "GALVIN LIKES LA CHANCE"!

WHAT? NO!

THAT MAKES IT SOUND LIKE THERE'S SOME KIND OF **HANKY PANKY** GOING ON!

OOOH! **IS** THERE?

OF **COURSE** NOT!!

SO YOU TWO KIDS DON'T HAVE A "RELATIONSHIP"?

NO! YOU'RE JUST MAKING STUFF **UP!!**

WINKA! WINKA!

THE NOTION THAT I HAVE A "RELATIONSHIP" WITH MS. LA CHANCE IS PURE **FANTASY!!**

OKAY, THANKS. I'VE GOT WHAT I NEED.

"GALVIN'S FANTASY: A RELATIONSHIP WITH LA CHANCE"

P.S. 38 WEEKLY BUGLE

IT'S AN EXCLUSIVE!

TIK TIK TIK

55

ALL RIGHT, GANG, SETTLE DOWN! WE'RE ABOUT TO MEET OUR "BOOK BUDDIES"!

YAK YAK YAK YAK YAK

MRS. BIGBEE'S CLASS IS EXCITED TO MEET YOU ALL!

NOK! NOK!

MRS. BIGBEE? HEY, SHE WAS **MY** FIRST GRADE TEACHER!!

✶CHUCKLE!✶ I WAS THE ONE WHO GAVE HER THE NICKNAME "MRS. BIG BUTT"!

HEL—... ...OHHH NO.

I THOUGHT THE OLD GAL WOULD BE **DEAD** BY NOW!

Peirce

REMEMBER ME, MRS. BIGBEE? NATE WRIGHT?

HOW COULD I FORGET?

BOY, THE OL' CLASSROOM HASN'T CHANGED MUCH SINCE **I** WAS IN FIRST GRADE!... OOP! THAT REMINDS ME!

GLUE

IS IT STILL HERE? IS IT... **YES!** IT **IS!**

ARE YOU OKAY?

JUST HAVING A FEW FLASHBACKS.

GUYS, SEE THIS DENT? MY **HEAD** MADE THAT!

ALL RIGHT, EVERYONE, PLEASE BE PATIENT AS WE PAIR EACH OF YOU WITH A "BOOK BUDDY"!

WHO AM **I** PAIRED WITH, MS. CLARKE?

I BELIEVE MRS. BIGBEE HAS SOMEONE IN MIND FOR YOU, NATE!

I DO INDEED, NATE! I'D LIKE YOU TO MEET...

PETER!

GAHH!

AH! YOU TWO **KNOW** EACH OTHER!

UNFORTUNATELY, YESH. ISH THISH SHOME KIND OF SHICK JOKE?

Peirce

MRS. BIGBEE, **SHURELY** THERE MUSHT BE SHOME **OTHER** SHIXTH GRADER WHO'LL BE MY "BOOK BUDDY"!

I'M ALREADY FAMILIAR WITH **THISH** ONE!

YOU ARE, PETER? HOW?

I ATTENDED HISH LAME EXCUSHE FOR A **SHUMMER** CAMP!

PARDONE AY **MWA**, PETER, BUT "CAMP NATE" WAS NOT **LAME**!

PLAYING "DUCK DUCK GOOSHE" WITH TWO PEOPLE ISHN'T LAME?

WELL, **SURE'** IT IS, WITH **THAT** SORT OF ATTI-TUDE!

Peirce

MR. EUSTIS! WHAT ARE YOU DOING?

RAKING LEAVES, OBVIOUSLY!

BUT YOU ALWAYS HIRE **ME** TO DO THAT!

I KNOW, NATE, BUT THAT WAS BEFORE I WENT ON MY DIET! I HAD NO ENERGY, NO STAMINA!

NOW I'M FIT ENOUGH TO DO IT MY**SELF**!

SO LET ME GET THIS STRAIGHT: YOU LOST ALL THIS WEIGHT...

RIGHT...

YOU FEEL GREAT... YOU LOOK LIKE A MILLION BUCKS...

✶AHEM!✶ WELL...

...AND YOU RE-WARD YOURSELF BY DOING **YARDWORK**?

ISN'T THERE A BETTER WAY OF CELEBRATING THE "NEW YOU"?

HI THERE.

LISTEN, PETER, IF WE'RE GOING TO BE "BOOK BUDDIES", WE'D BETTER GET TO WORK!

BUT I DON'T **NEED** A "BOOK BUDDY"!

DON'T YOU WANT TO LEARN TO READ?

I ALREADY **KNOW** HOW TO READ! I'M A **PROLIFIC** READER!

I HAPPEN TO BE HALFWAY THROUGH JAMESH JOYCE'SH "ULYSSHES"!

UH... THAT'S COOL, PETER, BUT NEXT TIME YOU SAY "JAMES JOYCE'S ULYSSES", COULD YOU TURN YOUR HEAD IN THE OTHER DIRECTION?

Peirce

OKAY, PETER, YOU'RE RIGHT. YOU'RE ALREADY SUCH A GOOD READER, YOU DON'T REALLY **NEED** A BOOK BUDDY.

...BUT I'LL TELL YOU WHAT YOU DO NEED: A **LITERARY ADVISOR**!

LITERARY ADVISHOR?

SOMEONE TO EXPAND YOUR HORIZONS! SOMEONE TO SHOW YOU THERE'S MORE TO LITERATURE THAN DUSTY OLD NOVELS!

FIVE SECONDS LATER...

SHE'S CALLED "FEMME FATALITY"!

COLOR ME SHMITTEN.

Peirce

COME **ON**! ARE WE GETTING TREATS OR **WHAT**?

YES! YES! JUST WAIT ONE MINUTE!

DAD! **MOVE** IT! THESE KIDS ARE GETTING UGLY!

HERE!... ☆GASP!☆... HERE'S ALL I COULD COME UP WITH!

HANG ON, GANG! HALLOWEEN TREATS COMIN' UP!

OKAY, WHO WANTS SOME BOUILLON CUBES?

GUYS?

GET THE EGGS, HUGHIE.

Peirce

MRS. GODFREY, HOW COME WE NEVER GET TREATS IN CLASS?

TREATS?

YEAH! BACK IN ELEMENTARY SCHOOL, WE GOT CANDY IF OUR BEHAVIOR WAS GOOD, OR IF WE DID WELL ON A TEST, OR...

✻SNORT!✻ I DON'T BELIEVE IN TRYING TO MOTIVATE STUDENTS BY BRIBING THEM WITH **FOOD**.

TRANSLATION: SHE DOESN'T WANT TO SHARE ANY OF THE "JUNIOR MINTS" SHE'S GOT HIDDEN IN HER DESK.

Peirce

YEAH, WHAT IS IT?

MISTER, WOULD YOU LIKE TO BUY A WALL HANGING TO SUPPORT THE JUNIOR WOODCHUCKS?

NO. GOOD-BYE.

WAIT, WAIT! I HAVEN'T SHOWN YOU THE BROCHURE YET!

LOOK! THEY'VE ALL GOT SAYINGS ON THEM!

NOT INTERESTED.

"HONESTY IS THE BEST POLICY." THAT'S A GOOD ONE! OR HOW ABOUT "CARPE DIEM"? I THINK THAT'S FRENCH!

THIS ONE'S NICE: "WELCOME TO OUR HOME".

JUST ABOUT ANY SAYING YOU CAN THINK OF, I'VE GOT IT!

HOW ABOUT "BEWARE OF DOG"?

♪

ACCORDING TO THIS ARTICLE, WOMEN ARE ATTRACTED TO "BAD BOYS"!

THERE'S SOMETHING ABOUT A REBEL THAT THE LADIES FIND IRRESISTIBLE! HMMM!...

COSMO

GENTS, I DO BELIEVE I'M GETTING ANOTHER BRILLIANT IDEA!

"ANOTHER"?

YUP! THE HITS JUST KEEP ON COMIN'!

A LEATHER JACKET?

HE'S A "BAD BOY".

YOU'RE ACTUALLY FOLLOWING THROUGH ON THAT DUMB IDEA?

DUMB IDEA? IT'S RIGHT HERE IN BLACK AND WHITE!

"FOR A MULTITUDE OF REASONS, WOMEN ARE OFTEN ATTRACTED TO "BAD BOYS" - MEN WHO SIMPLY AREN'T GOOD FOR THEM."

COSMO

THAT'S YOU, ALL RIGHT!

YEAH, YOU'RE GOOD FOR **NOTHING**!

HI, LADIES.

Peirce

CHESS
MEET
VS.
JEFFERSON
TODAY
3:30
ETERIA

I CAN'T BELIEVE YOU'RE THE NUMBER TWO PLAYER ON YOUR TEAM!

ON **OUR** TEAM YOU'D BE NO BETTER THAN NUMBER **SIX**! MAYBE **SEVEN**!

THERE! SEE? YOU JUST PROVED MY **POINT**! YOU WALKED RIGHT INTO MY **TRAP**!

CHECK! WHAT DO YOU SAY TO **THAT**?

HERE.

A **FORK**?

IT SHOULD COME IN HANDY...

...WHEN YOU EAT A BIG OL' SLICE OF HUMBLE PIE.

CHECKMATE.

GAWK!

BON APPÉTIT!

REMEMBER THAT SUB WE HAD LAST SPRING?

MRS. ESTERHAUS!

OH, YEAH! WAS **SHE** IN OVER HER HEAD!

FOR THREE DAYS WE DID NOTHING IN CLASS BUT PLAY "HANGMAN"! IT WAS **GREAT!**

THINK WE COULD GET HER BACK?

WELL, MAYBE. IF ONE OF THE **REAL** TEACHERS GOT SICK OR SOMETHING.

HMMM... RIGHT...

...AND BY THE WAY, THAT WAS JUST A STATEMENT OF FACT, NOT A...

FIRST, WE'LL NEED A DART GUN.

GUYS! OUR WISH CAME TRUE! I JUST HEARD MRS. GODFREY IS **SICK** TODAY!

YESSS!

WHO'S THE SUB? IS IT MRS. ESTERHAUS?

I'M NOT SURE! I **HOPE** SO!

HEY, EVEN IF IT'S **NOT** MRS. ESTERHAUS, WHO **CARES**? **ANY** SUB IS GOING TO BE A DAY TRIP TO FUN CITY!

AWRIGHT, SCRUBS! SIDDOWN AND **PACK IT!**

COACH JOHN!

COACH JOHN! WHAT ARE **YOU** DOING HERE?

WHAT DOES IT **LOOK** LIKE, SOLDIER? **SUBSTITUTE TEACHING!**

BUT YOU'RE A **GYM TEACHER!**

WHOA, SON! I CAN TEACH **ANYTHING!**

I'M AS COMFORTABLE IN A **CLASSROOM** AS I AM IN A **LOCKER** ROOM! I'M NOT JUST AN **ATHLETE!**

HE'S NOT JUST AN ATHLETE.

NOW **DROP AND GIVE ME TWENTY!!**

Peirce

YOU THERE! STOP YOUR YACKING!

YOU REMIND ME OF A KID I COACHED AT **SOCCER CAMP** LAST YEAR! YOU'RE JUST LIKE HIM: A SPIKY-HAIRED **CHATTER**BOX!

I REMEMBER HE PLAYED GOALIE, AND ONE DAY...

COACH JOHN! THAT WAS **ME!**

SEE? **BACK**TALK! GAD, YOU'RE LIKE HIS **TWIN!**

THIS GUY'S A FEW SLICES SHORT OF A LOAF.

SHEILA? WE HAVE A NEW STUDENT! MEET BECKY!

HI!

WILL YOU SHOW HER AROUND THE SCHOOL?

SURE! C'MON, BECKY!

THIS IS SMALLER THAN MY OLD SCHOOL!

YUP! WE'RE PRETTY TINY!

...BUT THAT'S NICE, BECAUSE YOU GET TO KNOW EVERYONE!

I KNOW EVERY SINGLE KID IN THE SIXTH GRADE PERSONALLY!

WOW!

WHO WAS THAT?

I HAVE NO IDEA.

I NOTICE A FEW OF YOU SCHOLARS ARE TRYING TO GET EXCUSED FROM CLASS BECAUSE YOU'RE "SICK"!

WELL, YOU DON'T EVEN KNOW WHAT SICK **IS**, SOLDIERS! YOU HAVE NO EARTHLY **IDEA**!

YOU WANT TO TALK **SICK**? TRY EATING A JAR OF RANCID MAYONNAISE AND THEN WATCHING "THE **EXORCIST**"!

NOW I REALLY **DO** NEED TO BE EXCUSED.

BUT ENOUGH "PLEDGE WEEK" STORIES...

COACH JOHN IS AN ABSOLUTE **PSYCHO**! I DON'T THINK I CAN STAND ANOTHER DAY OF HIM SUBBING!

YOU WON'T HAVE TO!

I JUST SAW MRS. GODFREY! SHE'S BACK!

SHE **IS**?

I DON'T THINK I'LL EAT TURKEY AGAIN AS LONG AS I **LIVE**!

BY MAKING ME EAT SO **MUCH** OF IT, MY DAD HAS **RUINED** A PERFECTLY GOOD FOOD FOR ME!

I ONCE THREW UP AFTER EATING A BUNCH OF GUMMI BEARS AND NOW I, LIKE, TOTALLY HATE GUMMI BEARS.

THANKS, TEDDY. WHAT A FASCINATING ADDITION TO THE DISCUSSION.

ONE BEAR CAME OUT MY NOSE.

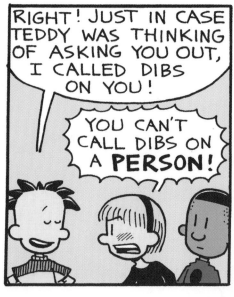

MR. GALVIN, I MISUNDERSTOOD YOU WHEN YOU TOLD ME TO WRITE A REPORT ON PLUTO.

PLEASE DON'T TELL ME YOU WROTE ABOUT THE DISNEY CHARACTER.

NO, NO! OF **COURSE** NOT!

I WROTE ABOUT THAT FAT GUY WHO'S ALWAYS TRYING TO BEAT UP POPEYE.

THAT'S "BLUTO", SON.

WAIT, WASN'T HE ALSO SOMETIMES CALLED "BRUTUS"?

THERE! SEE? NO **WONDER** I WAS CONFUSED!

Peirce

MRS. CZERWICKI, WHAT SORT OF MESSAGE ARE TEACHERS SENDING WHEN THEY DON'T TRUST US STUDENTS?

DETENTION
ROOM
IET, PLEASE

I ASKED TO BE EXCUSED FROM SOCIAL STUDIES BECAUSE I HAD A BLOODY NOSE, AND MRS. GODFREY DIDN'T **BELIEVE** ME!

AND **DID** YOU HAVE A BLOODY NOSE?

NO, I WAS JUST TRYING TO GET OUT OF CLASS.

BUT THE POINT IS, WHERE IS THE **TRUST**?

SIT DOWN, CHILD.

Peirce

WOW! COOL DRAWING!

I'VE BEEN WORKING ON IT ALL PERIOD!

THIS MAY VERY WELL BE THE BEST PIECE OF ART I'VE EVER MADE!

UNFORTUNATELY, YOU MADE IT DURING SOCIAL STUDIES.

...✺KOFF!✺... ..WHICH IS WHY IT'S A PICTURE OF THE GETTYS-BURG ADDRESS!

WITH NINJAS?

Peirce

HERE'S WHAT I DON'T GET, MRS. GODFREY: HOW AM I SUPPOSED TO PAY ATTENTION IN CLASS...

... WHEN YOU KEEP SENDING ME TO THE PRINCIPAL'S OFFICE **DURING** CLASS? YOU'RE NOT MAKING SENSE!

I'M A TEACHER. I DON'T **HAVE** TO MAKE SENSE.

ODDLY ENOUGH, EVERYTHING HAS JUST BECOME CRYSTAL CLEAR.

NCIPAL

Peirce

RRRRINNNGG!

THERE'S THE BELL.

JINX!

JINX!
JINX!
JINX!
JINX!

OWE ME A COKE!

OWE ME A COKE!
OWE ME A COKE!
OWE ME A COKE!
OWE ME A COKE!

FOOOO!...
GASP!
PANT
PANT PANT
WHEEZE

WHO WON?

IT WAS A TIE.

JINX!

SIGH...

I'M MAKING A LIST OF ALL THE UNFAIR ADVANTAGES TEACHERS HAVE OVER STUDENTS, MR. ROSA!

HM.

ITEM ONE: **YOU** GET TO USE AN **ELECTRIC** PENCIL SHARPENER WHILE **WE** USE THIS **CRANK** MODEL! THIS THING IS A TOTAL **DINOSAUR!**

I MEAN, YOU MIGHT AS WELL JUST MAKE US **WHITTLE** OUR PENCILS!

GREAT IDEA. STUDENTS WITH KNIVES.

THERE'S ITEM TWO: **YOU** GUYS GET TO USE **SARCASM!**

HERE'S ANOTHER INJUSTICE: YOU TEACH-ERS HAVE YOUR OWN **LOUNGE** TO HANG OUT IN! WE KIDS GET **NOTHING!**

WHERE ARE **WE** SUPPOSED TO HANG OUT?

"ARE THERE NO PRISONS? ARE THERE NO WORKHOUSES?"

THE HOLIDAYS DO STRANGE THINGS TO PEOPLE.

Peirce

I DON'T GET IT, DAD. WHAT'S YOUR PROBLEM WITH GETTING A DOG?

HOW ABOUT ALL THE **SHEDDING**?

I DON'T WANT TO SPEND THE REST OF MY LIFE SWEEPING UP **DOG HAIR**!

THE REST OF YOUR **LIFE**? ISN'T THAT A BIT **DRAMATIC**?

DOGS LIVE ABOUT TWELVE YEARS! THAT HARDLY BRINGS YOU TO THE END OF YOUR...

ACTUALLY, YOU'RE ALREADY PRETTY OLD, SO MAYBE...

GO PLAY OUTSIDE, BOY.

YOU DON'T WANT TO GET A DOG BECAUSE THEY **SHED**, RIGHT? WELL, I'VE BEEN RE-SEARCHING DOGS THAT **DON'T** SHED!

HOW ABOUT ONE OF THESE POODLE MIXES? WE COULD GET A LABRADOODLE! OR A SCHNOODLE!

HOW ABOUT A WESTIEPOO? WE COULD GET A WESTIEPOO!

IF I EVER GOT A DOG CALLED A "WESTIEPOO," I'D BE DRUMMED OUT OF MY THURSDAY NIGHT POKER GAME.

Peirce

'Twas the night before Christmas
When all through the house,
Not a creature was stirring

OPEN LATE XMAS eve

TIES
CLEARANCE

$

Not even a mouse.

PHEW!

129

LISTEN, WINK, SINCE I'VE GOT YOU ON THE PHONE, LET ME GIVE YOU SOME FEEDBACK ON LAST NIGHT'S FORECAST.

THAT BLUE BLAZER WASN'T REALLY DOING YOU ANY FAVORS, DUDE. IT MADE YOU LOOK A LITTLE PUDGY.

THEN AGAIN, YOU **ARE** A LITTLE PUDGY, WINK. I MEAN, YOU REALLY PACKED ON THE POUNDS AFTER THAT BABE WHO DOES THE MOVIE REVIEWS DUMPED YOU.

YOU'RE BETTER OFF WITHOUT HER, MAN. SHE ONLY GAVE **ONE STAR** TO "SNAKES ON A PLANE"!

HANG UP, WINK!

WHAT ARE YOU EATING, FRANCIS?

A PEANUT BUTTER AND POTATO CHIP SAND- WICH.

CRUNCH!

WHAT A GREAT IDEA!

YUP! I'VE BEEN DOING IT FOR YEARS!

WHOA! WHOA, BOY!

WHAT?

DON'T MAKE IT SOUND LIKE **YOU** INVENTED THE PEANUT BUTTER AND POTATO CHIP SANDWICH! **I** CAME UP WITH THAT IDEA!

YOU DID?

YES! BACK IN, LIKE, **SECOND GRADE!**

WHATEVER.

NO! **NO,** NOT "WHAT- EVER"! I WANT MY **CREDIT!**

I WANT THE WORLD TO KNOW JUST WHO INVENTED THE PEANUT BUTTER AND POTATO CHIP SANDWICH!

I STARTED EATING THEM BACK IN 1957!

FORGET EVERYTHING I JUST SAID.

CRUNCH!

I ALWAYS DO.

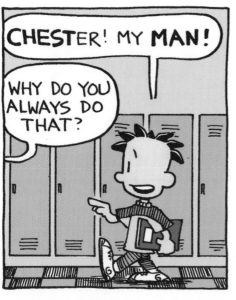

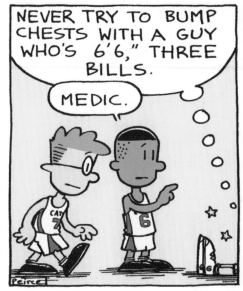

ALL RIGHT, FRANCIS, LET'S DISCUSS THE FACTS. HOW MUCH MONEY IS MISSING?

TWENTY BUCKS.

TWENTY DOLLARS. HMMM... AND NOW THAT MONEY HAS MYSTERIOUSLY DISAPPEARED, EH WHAT?

RIGHT.

HOW DO WE KNOW YOU DIDN'T TAKE IT?

WHAT? IT'S MY MONEY! WHY WOULD I STEAL FROM MY-SELF?

THE DEVIANT MIND IS OFTEN DIFFICULT TO UNDERSTAND.

... SAID THE KID WEARING A SHERLOCK HOLMES COSTUME AND SMOKING A BUBBLE PIPE.

FRANCIS! I HEARD YOU HAD SOME MONEY STOLEN!

NEVER FEAR, SHEILA! THE CULPRIT **WILL** BE CAUGHT!

I'M CURRENTLY CONDUCTING AN EXHAUSTIVE INVESTIGATION OF FRANCIS' LOCKER, WHICH WILL UNDOUBTEDLY YIELD A **MULTITUDE** OF VITAL INFORMATION!

UH... THAT'S **MY** LOCKER.

FOR A DETECTIVE, HE'S SURPRISINGLY CLUELESS.

OH, I'M NOT SURPRISED.

HI.

Peirce

JENNY, M'LADY!

WHAT'S UP, DORKUS?

MERELY A LITTLE SLEUTHING, MY DEAR! OUR FRIEND FRANCIS HAD SOME MONEY STOLEN FROM HIS LOCKER THIS MORNING!

MAY I ASK YOU A FEW QUESTIONS?

WHAT-EVER.

DO YOU FIND MEN IN CAPES SEXY?

CRIPES.

GO, SPITSY! GO!

WURF!

WHAT'S UP?

SPITSY IS UN-LOCKING THE PREDATOR WITHIN!

WHADDA YA MEAN?

TEDDY, WHAT'S THE NATURAL ENEMY OF DOGS? **DUH!** IT'S **CATS!**

WELL, EARLIER I SAW A CAT IN THE VACANT LOT! SO I SENT SPITSY IN THAT DIRECTION!

YOU THINK HE'LL TRACK IT DOWN?

OF **COURSE** HE WILL! HIS NATURAL CANINE IN-STINCTS WILL KICK IN!

BELIEVE YOU ME, SPITSY WILL FIND THAT CAT!

WHEN YOU'RE RIGHT, YOU'RE RIGHT!

CRIPES.

!

IS THE PRINCIPAL HERE, MRS. SHIPULSKI? I NEED TO REPORT A DISTURBING INCIDENT.

OH, DEAR.

I'M NOT AT LIBERTY TO DISCUSS IT, BUT SUFFICE IT TO SAY MY **WARDROBE** WILL PROVIDE YOU WITH SOME CLUES ABOUT THE MATTER!

I UNDERSTAND, NATE. SAY NO MORE. I'LL GET PRINCIPAL NICHOLS.

THANK YOU, MY DEAR.

SIR, NATE WRIGHT IS BEING TEASED FOR WEARING A CAPE AND A STRANGE HAT.

WHAT? NO!

Peirce

WHAT KIND OF A PERSON STEALS MONEY?

MOREOVER, WHAT KIND OF A PERSON STEALS MONEY FROM A **KID**? RIGHT OUT OF HIS **LOCKER**?

CLEARLY, I'M DEALING WITH A DERANGED INDIVIDUAL... A SICK MIND... A BORDERLINE PSYCHOPATH.

WELCOME TO MY WORLD.

THE PRIME SUSPECT, OBVIOUSLY, IS MRS. GODFREY.

WHAT'S UP, INSPECTOR GADGET?

MOCK ME IF YOU WANT, FRANCIS, BUT I'M ABOUT TO CATCH YOUR **THIEF**!

HA! RACHEL! I'VE CAUGHT YOU RED-HANDED!

RED-HAND..? **WHAT**?

I'VE BEEN STAKING OUT FRANCIS' LOCKER, KNOWING FULL WELL THAT WHOEVER **BURGLARIZED** IT THIS MORNING WOULD RETURN TO THE SCENE OF THE CRIME!

SPEAKING OF CRIMES, WHO DRESSED YOU?

I'M AFRAID, MY DEAR, THAT A FRISKING IS IN ORDER.

ROWR!

Peirce

I'M HANDING BACK YOUR TESTS, PEOPLE!

I THINK IT'S SAFE TO SAY THEY ARE AN ACCURATE REFLECTION OF YOUR EFFORTS...

...OR **LACK** THEREOF!

SOME OF YOU CLEARLY STUDIED HARD AND WERE VERY WELL-PREPARED...

OTHERS RECEIVED PASSING GRADES, BUT ARE CAPABLE OF DOING MUCH BETTER...

...AND THE REST OF YOU? WELL, ALL I CAN SAY IS...

...PERHAPS YOUR GRADE WILL SERVE AS A **WAKE-UP CALL!**

A WAKE-UP CALL!

Z

FIRE

153

FRANCIS! YO MAMA SMACK-DOWN!

HUH? WHAT ARE YOU TALKING ABOUT?

I DROP A "YO MAMA" ON YOU... YO MAMA'S SO FAT, WHEN SHE GETS ON AN ELEVATOR, SHE HAS TO GO DOWN!

...AND NOW YOU COME BACK AT ME!

WAIT, WAIT... MY MOTHER IS ACTUALLY QUITE SLENDER.

NO, NO, NO.

MAYBE YOU'RE THINKING OF TEDDY'S MOM!

WHAT? HEY!

ARTUR! YO MAMA SMACK-DOWN!

GOOD! YES! WHAT IS?

JUST LISTEN: YO MAMA'S SO UGLY...

EXCUSE PLEASE, NATE. SHOULD NOT IT BE "**YOUR** MAMA"?

WELL... YEAH, BUT THIS IS, LIKE, SLANG.

AH! "SLANG" IS LIKE NICK-NAME, YES? WE FIND NICKNAME FOR TO MY MOTHER!

ARTUR, TRY TO STAY ON TASK.

HOW ABOUT "CUBBY"?

156

WHAT'S UP, GENTS?

I'M TRYING TO TEACH ARTUR THE FINER POINTS OF THE YO MAMA SMACKDOWN.

AM NOT DOING GOOD SO FAR.

JUST WATCH ME, ARTUR! JUST DO WHAT I DO!

I'LL THROW DOWN SOME **KILLER** YO MAMAS AT THE NEXT PERSON TO COME AROUND THE CORNER!

THIS OUGHTA BE GOOD!

CH-CHESTER!

WHUT?

HELLO?

NATE? THIS IS MRS. GODFREY.

UH... HI.

MAY I SPEAK TO YOUR FATHER, PLEASE?

DAD?... ※ KOFF! ※ IT'S MRS. GODFREY.

YOUR TEACHER?

HELLO?

YES! HELLO, MRS. GODFREY!

OH, REALLY? NO, I **HADN'T** HEARD ABOUT THAT! HOW INTERESTING!

MM HMM... YES, THAT **DOES** SOUND LIKE SOMETHING HE SHOULD HAVE MENTIONED!

I WILL!... I CERTAINLY WILL!... YES, YOU CAN BE SURE OF THAT!... THANK YOU FOR CALLING.

BOOP!

SHE WAS JUST ASKING ME TO HELP CHAPERONE A FIELD TRIP, BUT **HE** DOESN'T HAVE TO KNOW THAT.

CAN I GET YOU ANYTHING?

Peirce

I JUST FINISHED THAT "FEMME FATALITY," NATE. BEST ISSUE **EVER**!

REALLY?

AFTER THE WOLF WARS IN THE KIEL GALAXY, FEMME RETURNS TO EARTH IN THE YEAR 2140!

...AND BECAUSE THE AVERAGE TEMPERATURE IS OVER ONE HUNDRED DEGREES, SHE SPENDS THE ENTIRE STORY... ✺AHEM!✺ ...DRESSED ACCORDINGLY!

I NEVER THOUGHT I'D SAY THIS, BUT... GOD BLESS GLOBAL WARMING!

AMEN, BROTHER!

HOO BOY.

LOOK, DAD, "FEMME FATALITY" IS **MY** CRUSH! CAN'T YOU GET A CRUSH OF YOUR **OWN**!?

DON'T YOU LIKE KATIE COURIC? GO DROOL OVER KATIE COURIC!

KATIE COURIC?

BUT... SINCE SHE LEFT "TODAY," THE SPARK IS GONE.

MOVE ALONG, DAD.

Peirce

MR. GALVIN?

207

NOK NOK

YES! HELLO THERE, NATE!

HI.

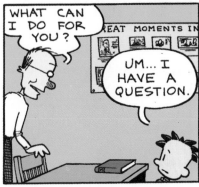
WHAT CAN I DO FOR YOU?

UM... I HAVE A QUESTION.

GREAT MOMENTS IN

ABOUT THE HOME-WORK?

NO, IT... IT'S SORT OF HARD TO ASK.

NOW DON'T BE SHY, MY BOY! WHATEVER YOUR QUESTION, I'M SURE I CAN ANSWER IT!

AFTER ALL, I'M HERE TO HELP!

WELL... OKAY...

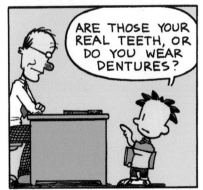
ARE THOSE YOUR REAL TEETH, OR DO YOU WEAR DENTURES?

CRIPES.

SAY DENTURES. I'VE GOT A DOLLAR RIDING ON THIS.

CANDY CORN? WHERE'D YOU GET CANDY CORN?

IT'S MINE. I'VE BEEN SAVING IT SINCE HALLOWEEN.

HALLO-WEEN?

I MAKE MY HALLOWEEN CANDY LAST UNTIL VALENTINE'S DAY, MY VALENTINE'S CANDY LAST UNTIL EASTER...

...AND THEN I MAKE MY **EASTER** CANDY LAST UNTIL HALLOWEEN! I'VE GOT THE WHOLE YEAR COVERED!

IMPRESSIVE, YET FREAKISH.

YUMMY, YET STALE.

CRUNCH!

Peirce

SO FOR THE PAST THREE MONTHS YOU'VE BEEN HOARDING HALLOWEEN CANDY!

NOT **HOARDING**. MAKING IT **LAST**!

YOU NEVER **SHARED** ANY OF IT, RIGHT? YOU NEVER OFFERED **ME** ANY! THAT MEANS IT **IS** HOARDING!

O**KAY**, OKAY! I'LL GIVE YOU SOME-THING!

WHAT'S THIS?

MY NEIGHBOR IS AN ORTHO-DONTIST.

DENTAL FLOSS ISN'T CANDY!

IT'S MINT-FLAVORED. ENJOY.

LA TA DEE DUM DAH...

YOU HAVEN'T THROWN OUT A RUNNER AT SECOND IN ALL OUR YEARS IN LITTLE LEAGUE.

WHAT'S UP, AMIGO?

I'M MAKING A VALENTINE FOR SHEILA.

OOH! LET ME TAKE A LOOK! I'LL GIVE YOU MY PROFESSIONAL OPINION!

PROFESSIONAL OPINION?

FRANCIS, I'M THE **KING** OF HOMEMADE VALENTINES! REMEMBER THE CARD I MADE FOR JENNY LAST YEAR? THE ONE WITH THE POEM?

"JENNY, JENNY, JENNY, JENNY. YOU SLAY ME LIKE SOUTH PARK'S KENNY."

AN INSTANT CLASSIC!

You've known me now
For many years,
But never have we dated.

For reasons
I don't understand,
You think our love ill-fated.

But Jenny,
I'm your destiny.
One day we will be mated.

And then you'll know
Just what it's like
To say that you've been "Nated."

JENNY, I WANT YOU TO KNOW THAT I UNDERSTAND WHY YOU DIDN'T GIVE ME A VALENTINE THIS YEAR!

OH?

IT'S BECAUSE YOU'RE **SCARED** OF **LIKING** ME TOO MUCH! IT'S EASIER TO **DENY** YOUR FEELINGS THAN TO **ADMIT** THEM!

THOSE SORTS OF POWERFUL EMOTIONS CAN BE OVER-WHELMING!

SO CAN NAUSEA.

NOW, NOW, MY SWEET! WE CALL THAT "LOVE-SICKNESS"!

WHAT ARE WE DOING IN ART TODAY, MR. ROSA?

MAKING A MESS.

TURNING MY CLASSROOM INTO AN ABSOLUTE PIGSTY THAT'LL TAKE THREE HOURS TO CLEAN UP AFTER SCHOOL, MAKING MY BACK EVEN MORE SORE THAN IT ALREADY **IS**!

MR. ROSA?

CLAY SCULPTURE.

YES!

I NEED AN ASPIRIN.

Peirce

YESSS! **CLAY!** CLAY IS MY FAVORITE ART PROJECT OF THE YEAR!

REMEMBER THAT **DRAGON** I MADE LAST YEAR? **THAT,** IF I DO SAY SO MYSELF, BELONGED IN A **MUSEUM!**

I'M A **MASTER** OF SCULPTURE! I'M THE **MICHELANGELO** OF SCULPTURE!

DUDE. MICHELANGELO WAS THE MICHELANGELO OF SCULPTURE.

WAS. PAST TENSE.

BAM BAM BAM BAM BAM

MICHELANGELO SAID THAT IN EVERY BLOCK OF MARBLE, THERE'S A HUMAN FORM STRUGGLING TO GET OUT!

WELL, SAME THING WITH THIS HUNK OF CLAY! INSIDE IT IS A HUMAN FORM STRUGGLING TO GET OUT!

THAT'S QUITE A STRUGGLE.

NICE MANATEE!

HI, MAY I SPEAK TO CHIEF METEOROLOGIST WINK SUMMERS, PLEASE?

WINK! NATE WRIGHT HERE!

GOOD FORECAST LAST NIGHT, WINK! YOU ACTUALLY GOT IT **RIGHT** FOR A CHANGE!

LISTEN, THOUGH, I DON'T THINK YOU SHOULD WEAR THAT TWEED BLAZER ANYMORE. IT JUST CALLS ATTENTION TO HOW FAT YOU ARE.

PLUS, YOU GOT A LITTLE TONGUE-TIED DURING THE RADAR SEGMENT. I WAS LIKE: WHAT'S UP WITH WINK TONIGHT? IS HE **DRUNK?**

BUT THAT'S NOT WHY I'M CALLING, WINK. I'M CALLING TO LET YOU KNOW THAT SOMETHING MIGHTY FUNKY IS GOING ON WITH YOUR "HAIR REPLACEMENT SYSTEM."

IT LOOKS BAD. FRANKLY, IT LOOKS LIKE THERE'S A...

BEEP!

HE PUT A TIME LIMIT ON HIS ANSWERING MACHINE, SO NOW I HAVE TO LEAVE MY MESSAGES IN ONE-MINUTE CHUNKS.

boop boop boop boop boop

I'M GUESSING HE ALSO HAS "CALLER I.D."

...LIKE THERE'S A DEAD CAT LYING ON YOUR HEAD.

DON'T YOU THINK IT'S KIND OF WEIRD THAT NATE IS SUCH A CHESS PHENOM?

I MEAN, YOU'D EXPECT SOMEONE WHO'S SO GOOD AT CHESS TO BE, LIKE, REALLY **SMART**, RIGHT?

BUT HE'S JUST THE **OPPOSITE!** HE'S **CLUELESS!** MOST OF THE TIME HE HAS NO IDEA WHAT'S GOING **ON!**

NO OFFENSE.

HUH?

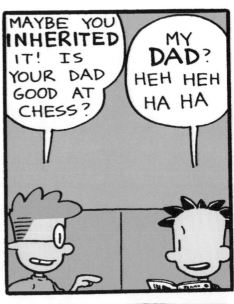

WHAT'S WITH THE CAMERA?

I'VE JOINED THE YEARBOOK STAFF! I'M IN CHARGE OF CANDIDS!

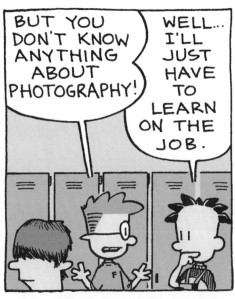

BUT YOU DON'T KNOW ANYTHING ABOUT PHOTOGRAPHY!

WELL... I'LL JUST HAVE TO LEARN ON THE JOB.

YOU NEED A MENTOR.

YES!... A MENTOR! AND I KNOW JUST THE PERSON!

RRINNG!

MOTHER! PHONE!

FIRE TORPEDOES, MISTER SULU.

AYE, CAPTAIN.

pierce

SCHOOL PICTURE GUY! IN THE FLESH, KID! THE MASTER HAS ARRIVED TO TUTOR THE APPRENTICE!

SO YOU'VE DECIDED TO BE A PHOTOGRAPHER, MY LAD! AN ADMIRABLE PROFESSION! A NOBLE CALLING!

HOW WELL I REMEMBER WHEN **I** WAS FIRST BITTEN BY THE SHUTTER BUG! YES, AMIGO, I RECALL IT **VIVIDLY!**

STORY TIME.

HEADS TURNED THE DAY I VENTURED UNCERTAINLY INTO THE YEARBOOK MEETING...

TAKE A LOOK, KID! EVERYWHERE AROUND YOU, THERE ARE **MOMENTS** HAPPENING! THEY HAPPEN, AND THEN THEY'RE **GONE!**

AS A PHOTOGRAPHER, THOUGH, **YOU** HAVE THE POWER TO MAKE THOSE MOMENTS LIVE **FOREVER!!**

THAT'S THE NUMBER ONE GOAL OF TAKING GOOD CANDIDS, KID: CAPTURING A MOMENT IN TIME!

I THOUGHT THE NUMBER ONE GOAL WAS CATCHING PEOPLE WITH STUPID LOOKS ON THEIR FACES.

TRUE. BUT WE DON'T SPEAK OF THAT.

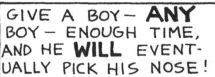

I SHOT A WHOLE ROLL OF CANDIDS, AND ALL OF THEM ARE BOR-ING.

ARE YOU **KIDDING**? MY LAD, THIS IS A **GOLD** MINE!

YOU'RE FORGETTING THE SECRET OF YEARBOOK CANDIDS: IT'S ALL ABOUT THE **CAPTION**!

SLAP THE PROPER CAPTION UNDERNEATH THIS ORDINARY PHOTO OF MRS. GODFREY, AND WE'RE TALKIN' **MAGIC**!

HOW ABOUT "▇▇▇▇ ▇▇▇▇▇ ▇▇▇▇"?

GOOD! TOTALLY IN-APPROPRIATE, BUT GOOD!

FORTUNE COOKIE?

THAT REMAINS TO BE SEEN.

KRAK!

WHADDA YA MEAN?

ARRGH! **THIS** IS WHAT I MEAN!

THIS IS **NOT A FORTUNE!** IT'S JUST SOME LAME **SAYING!**

A FORTUNE IS SUPPOSED TO TELL YOU, "ONE DAY YOU'LL BE RICH" OR "TODAY WILL BE YOUR LUCKY DAY"! IT'S SUPPOSED TO PREDICT THE **FUTURE!**

DOES THIS PREDICT THE FUTURE? **NO!** SO IT'S NOT A **FORTUNE!** CALLING 'EM "FORTUNE COOKIES" IS **WRONG!**

HERE, **YOU** TAKE IT! I DON'T **WANT** IT!

!

TRIP!

"YOU ARE EASILY ANNOYED BY MATTERS OF LITTLE CONSEQUENCE."

WHO PUT **THAT** THERE?

NATE, I UNDERSTAND YOU WERE DISRUPTIVE IN MRS. GODFREY'S CLASS.

I JUST CRACKED A LITTLE JOKE IS ALL!

IT WAS INAPPROPRIATE.

I'M A **KIDDER**, THAT'S ALL! I LIKE TO JOKE AROUND! THAT'S NOT INAPPROPRIATE!

I MEAN, IS IT INAPPROPRIATE WHEN I KID WITH **YOU** ABOUT YOUR MORBID OBESITY?

✳ SIGH... ✳

OF **COURSE** NOT! BECAUSE FAT PEOPLE ARE SO **JOLLY**!

PAT PAT

Peirce

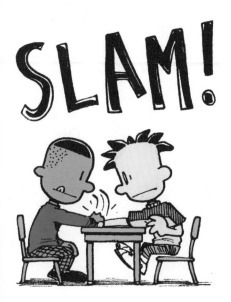

MRS. GODFREY, CAN TEDDY AND I BE PARTNERS FOR THE CIVIL WAR REPORT?

I DON'T THINK SO, NATE.

BUT YOU **NEVER** LET US WORK TOGETHER!

THAT'S NOT TRUE.

I LET THE TWO OF YOU PAIR UP LAST YEAR FOR YOUR PAPER ON GIOVANNI DA VERRAZANO!

WHO?

SOUNDS FRENCH.

YOU'RE MAKING MY POINT, BOYS.

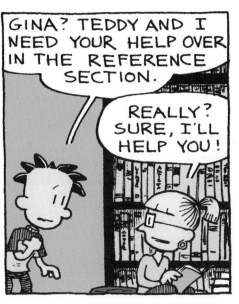

HOW DID YOU DOLTS COME UP WITH SUCH A GOOD TOPIC? YOU DIDN'T EVEN CRACK A **BOOK!**

EASY! TEDDY'S DAD IS A CIVIL WAR BUFF!

HE'S BEEN TELLING ME ABOUT ALL THE DIFFERENT BATTLES SINCE I WAS A BABY! HE BUILDS MODELS OF CIVIL WAR BATTLEFIELDS IN OUR BASEMENT!

I COULD WRITE A REPORT ON THE BATTLE OF SHILOH IN MY **SLEEP!**

...WHICH IS WHY I CHOSE HIM AS MY PARTNER!

RIGHT, AND... WAIT. WHAT?

RELAX, DUDE. WE'LL PUT YOUR NAME FIRST ON THE TITLE PAGE.

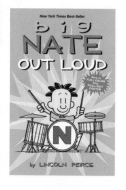
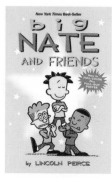
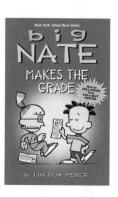

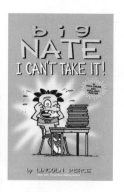
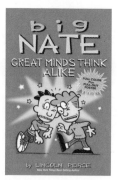
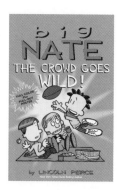
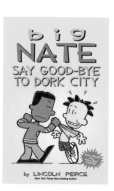
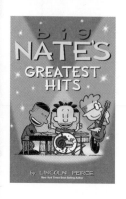

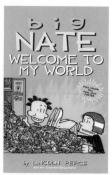